EBENEZER STONES

EBENEZER STONES

USING AN ORDINARY STONE TO REMIND YOU OF OUR EXTRAORDINARY GOD

Study Guide

Seven Weeks

CATHERINE MCDAUGALE

with MARIE TAYLOR

WALK BY FAITH
MEDIA

Then Samuel took a stone and set it up between Mizpah and Shen, and called its name Ebenezer, saying, "Thus far the LORD has helped us."

— 1 Samuel 7:12 (NKJV)

CONTENTS

How to Use This Study Guide.. i

Week 1: REMEMBERING GOD'S FAITHFULNESS 1

Week 2: BECOMING A CHILD OF GOD.................................... 11

Week 3: GROWING IN SPIRITUAL MATURITY.......................... 23

Week 4: THE GOOD SHEPHERD 35

Week 5: YIELDING TO THE GOOD SHEPHERD...................... 47

Week 6: DOING GOD'S WORK.. 59

Week 7: WALKING BY FAITH WITH GOD 71

Streaming Video Access.. 83

HOW TO USE THIS STUDY GUIDE

This study guide is designed to be used with the book *Ebenezer Stones: using an ordinary stone to remind you of our extraordinary God* to help you see God's faithfulness in your life. His faithfulness permeates our lives. Yet, sometimes we forget. Our minds get consumed by our circumstances, problems, and desires—leaving no room to think about what God has done for us.

But God wants us to remember. He wants us to meditate on all of the amazing things he has done in our lives.

When we take time to focus our thoughts on how God has been faithful and set up memorials, God gets the glory. Seeing those Ebenezer stones then reminds us to think about His faithfulness. And when we do, we're encouraged.

Over the course of seven weeks, you will be able to

- internalize what the Bible tells us about God's faithfulness;

- recognize the ways God has been faithful to you; and

- set up your own memorials.

This study guide can be used by individuals, a Bible study group, or any small group gathering. Each week is broken into five days of study, with prompts about which portion of the book to read, a Bible verse to memorize, questions to help you apply what you've learned, and space to journal about what God is teaching you.

If you're meeting as a group, each person should have copies of the study guide and book. As you go through the study, complete the material before meeting as a group. Doing so will help facilitate the discussion during your group time.

Regardless of whether you're going through the study on your own or as part of a group, the following steps will help you get the most out of the study:

Step 1: Begin each day of study with prayer, asking God to show you what He wants you to learn about His faithfulness. The Holy Spirit teaches us all things. So, put your heart and mind in the right perspective to prepare to receive from Him.

Step 2: As you read, note or highlight the portions of the book and study guide that stand out to you. When you do, you'll be able to quickly go back to the parts of the book and study guide that you would like to discuss in your study group.

Step 3: Write down any questions you have. You can go back to those questions during your group study time or reach out to your pastor or a leader at your church.

Step 4: Journal about how God is speaking to you. Space will be provided on Day 5 of each week for this purpose. Taking the time to record the things God shows you during the study will help you to internalize them.

Step 5: Make sure you take the time to answer all of the questions. The questions in the study will help you to internalize the information you read in the book each week. And, if you're part of a study group, answering them ahead of time will make your group time more meaningful for everyone.

Step 6: Practice memorizing the memory verses. By hiding God's Word in your heart, you'll have it with you wherever you go. And you'll be able to meditate on it no matter where you are or what you're doing.

The exercises in this study guide use the New Living Translation and the New Kings James Version. However, feel free to memorize the verses in the version you are comfortable using.

Throughout the week, ask a friend, your children, or your spouse to test you. This will both help you to memorize the verse and be an influencer in seeking after the things of God.

Step 7: At the end of each week, take time to record how God has been faithful in your life.

Memorials of God's faithfulness can take on various forms. If you don't already have a method of documenting God's faithfulness in your life, here are some ideas to get you started.

1. Start an Ebenezer stones jar.

One way to memorialize God's faithfulness is with an Ebenezer stones jar and actual stones. You can use any jar or container that you like. Then find or buy some stones.

Use a permanent or a paint marker to write the date of the event on one side and a few words that will jog your memory about how God helped you on the other side. Then place the stone in the jar or container that you've set aside for this purpose.

Put your Ebenezer stones jar in a place where you will see it every day. When you see it, take some time to reflect on the stones you've placed in the jar.

2. Start a blessing jar.

A blessing jar is similar to an Ebenezer stones jar. The difference is that you'll use small pieces of paper instead of stones. When God helps you in some way during your day or week, write it down on a piece of paper with the date and put it in the jar.

This method of recording God's faithfulness works well as a family activity. When God helps someone in your household, have them write it down and put it in the blessing jar. Then at the end of the week or month, spend time as a family reflecting on how God has been working in your lives.

3. Start a journal.

Another way to record God's faithfulness is by writing down the things God has done for you—the ways He has helped you—in a journal. This is the most thorough way to document His faithfulness. Take time to memorialize all aspects of the event, including the way you felt before and after God worked in your life.

If you choose this method, find a place to display your journal somewhere in your home so you will still have a visual reminder of God's faithfulness. If you put it in a drawer somewhere, you won't get the same encouragement as you do when you can see it every day.

4. Start a prayer journal.

Finally, you could start a journal that's dedicated to your prayers. When you open the journal, write your prayers on the left side with the date, leaving the right side blank. As God answers your prayers, big or small, take time to go back and write God's answer with the date on the right side.

Then take time every month or so to look through the journal and meditate on how God has answered your prayers. It's a great reminder that God is always there for you, listening when you call to Him, and helping you in His will and timing.

You can do one of these or a combination of them. Journaling will make a more complete record of how God has helped you throughout your life. And it could even become a legacy that you leave behind. One day, we will all go to be with the Lord. Your journal could then have the effect of encouraging others.

And if you don't like these ideas, come up with your own. The important thing is to find a way to remind yourself about God's faithfulness in your life. Because He is faithful every day.

Praying that you will be blessed as you go through the study and remember all of the ways God has been faithful to you!

WEEK 1

REMEMBERING GOD'S FAITHFULNESS

God is always faithful. No matter where you've been or what you've done, God's faithfulness remains steadfast, unmovable, and constant. Every day, He's there, working in your life.

This study is about remembering the ways God has been faithful to you. It's not about nostalgia—getting caught up in memories and wishing you could go back to that time. Instead, it's about reminding yourself of how God has helped you.

The focus should be on what God can do, not on what you've done or what has happened to you. When you meditate on God's ability to work in and through your life, it will build up your faith and trust in Him.

In the first week of the study, you will go through the *Introduction* and chapter 1. As you read, think about the ways God has been faithful to you.

Day 1

Pray and read the Introduction. Then answer the following questions based on what you've read.

1. How often do you take time to focus on the Lord?

   ☐ Daily

   ☐ Three or more times per week

   ☐ Once a week

   ☐ Monthly

   ☐ Only when I need to

2. How easy is it for you to recognize God's faithfulness?

   _____

   _____

   _____

   _____

3. List some recent ways God has . . .

Guided you: _____

_____

_____

_____

Redirected you: _____

_____

_____

Protected you: _____

_____

_____

_____

Helped you: _____

_____

_____

Provided for you: _____

_____

_____

_____

Memorize Scripture. Write out Philippians 4:8 (NLT).

_____

_____

_____

_____

_____

Day 2

Pray and read chapter 1, pages 1 to 3 (stopping at the end of the first full paragraph). Then answer the following questions based on what you've read.

1. In 1 Samuel 7:12, what did Samuel say the Ebenezer stone set up between Mizpah and Shen represented?

    _____

    _____

2. Before that, the Israelites had set up stones in the Jordan River. Joshua told us why they were set up. What was the reason he gave?_____

    _____

    _____

3. How do you currently keep track of God's faithfulness in your life?_____

    _____

    _____

    _____

    _____

4. Think of those who may be watching you live out your faith. What evidence of your faith will they be able to point to when you leave this earth? _____

    _____

    _____

    _____

    _____

    _____

Memorize Scripture. Fill in the missing words to Philippians 4:8 (NLT).

> "And now, dear brothers and _____, one final thing. _____ your _____ on what is _____, and honorable, and _____ and pure, and _____, and admirable. _____ about things that are excellent and _____ of praise."

Day 3

Pray and read chapter 1, page 3 (starting at the second full paragraph) to page 4 (stopping at the end of the third full paragraph). Then answer the following questions based on what you've read.

1. Why do we have times when we doubt that God is faithful? _____

   _____

2. In those times of doubt, what are we doing instead of meditating on who God is? _____

   _____

   _____

3. Do you currently have circumstances in your life that are causing you to worry and doubt that God can help you? Write them out here and pray over them. _____

   _____

   _____

   _____

   _____

   _____

   _____

Memorize Scripture. Fill in more missing words to Philippians 4:8 (NLT).

"And _____, dear brothers and _____, one _____ thing. _____ your _____ on what is _____, and honorable, and _____, and pure, and _____, and admirable. _____ about things that are _____ and _____ of praise."

Day 4

Pray and read chapter 1, page 4 (starting at the last paragraph) to page 6. Then answer the *Going Deeper* questions on pages 6 to 9.

Going Deeper 1. _____

_____

_____

_____

Going Deeper 2. _____

_____

_____

_____

Going Deeper 3. _____

_____

_____

_____

_____

_____

Going Deeper 4. _____

_____

_____

_____

_____

_____

Memorize Scripture. Finish each word in this week's verse.

"A____ n____, d_____ b_____ a____ s_____,

o____ f_____ t_____. F____ y_____ t_____

o___ w_____ i___ t_____, a____ h_____,

a____ r_____, a____ p_____, a____ l_____,

a____ a_____. T_____ a_____ t_____

t_____ a____ e_____ a____ w_____

o__ p_____." (P_____ 4:____ (NLT))

Day 5

Memorize Scripture. Using the first letter of each word in Philippians 4:8 (NLT) (*see* below), write out the verse from memory.

_____

_____

_____

_____

_____

"A n, d b a s, o f t. F y t o w i t, a h, a r, a p, a l, a a. T a t t a e a w o p."

Chapter Notes. Pray and take time to meditate on what God has shown you this week. Journal about what stood out to you and about one way that God has been faithful to you in your life.

_____

_____

_____

_____

_____

_____

WEEK 2

BECOMING A CHILD OF GOD

God wants you to be His child. He wants to have a relationship with you. As you start the second week of the study, reflect on where you stand in relation to God. Have you accepted His free gift of salvation?

In chapter 2, we'll reflect on the most amazing way that God has been faithful to us. He made a way for us to have our sins forgiven. God Himself made the ultimate sacrifice so we could become His children.

Day 1

Pray and read chapter 2, pages 11 to 15 (stopping before the heading, *My Ebenezer Stone of Salvation*). Then answer the following questions based on what you've read.

1. Who cannot fully appreciate the faithfulness of God?

   _____

   _____

2. Define what it means to be a creation of God. _____

   _____

   _____

   _____

3. Define what it means to be a child of God. _____

   _____

   _____

   _____

4. What did Adam and Eve enjoy with God in the Garden of Eden? _____

   _____

   _____

5. How did Adam and Eve break their relationship with God? _____

   _____

   _____

   _____

6. What plan did God have for sin? _____

   _____

   _____

   _____

   _____

   _____

   Who could fulfill God's plan? _____

   _____

   _____

Memorize Scripture. Write out 2 Corinthians 5:21 (NLT).

   _____

   _____

   _____

   _____

   _____

Day 2

Pray and read chapter 2, page 15 (starting at the heading, *My Ebenezer Stone of Salvation*) to page 18. Then answer the following questions based on what you've read.

1. How long did God wait for the author to fully surrender her life to Him? _____

   And how long did God wait for *you* to fully surrender your life to Him? _____

2. What were the circumstances in your life that finally brought you to the end of yourself? _____

   _____

   _____

   _____

   _____

   _____

   _____

3. What promise does God fulfill when you search for Him with all your heart? _____

   _____

   _____

4. What does fully seeking God mean to you? _____

_____

_____

_____

_____

_____

5. How would you describe who Jesus is to you? _____

_____

_____

_____

_____

_____

_____

Memorize Scripture. Fill in the missing words to 2 Corinthians 5:21 (NLT).

"For _____ made Christ, who _____ sinned, to be the _____ for our _____, so that we could be made _____ with _____ through Christ."

Day 3

Pray and read chapter 2, pages 19 to 21. Then answer the following questions based on what you've read.

1. Who set the standards of the 10 commandments? ___

    _____

    _____

2. Have you been able to keep all of God's 10 commandments? _____

    Which commandment stumbles you the most and why? _____

    _____

    _____

    _____

3. What is God's gift of salvation? _____

    _____

    _____

    _____

    _____

    _____

Through whom do you receive that gift? _____

_____

_____

4. Can a person be forgiven of sin and reconciled to God
   after dying? _____

   What happens instead? _____

   _____

   _____

5. According to 2 Peter 3:9, what does God not want to
   happen to anyone? _____

   _____

   _____

6. What is someone doing by "calling on His name"?

   _____

   _____

   _____

   _____

   _____

   _____

   _____

Memorize Scripture. Fill in more missing words to 2 Corinthians 5:21 (NLT).

"For _____ made _____, who _____

_____, to be the _____ for our

_____, so that _____ could be _____ _____

with _____ through _____."

Day 4

Pray and answer the ***Going Deeper*** questions on pages 21 to 23.

Going Deeper 1. _____

_____

_____

_____

_____

_____

_____

_____

_____

_____

Going Deeper 2. _____

_____

_____

_____

_____

_____

Going Deeper 3. _____

_____

_____

_____

_____

_____

_____

_____

Memorize Scripture. Finish each word in this week's verse.

"F___ G_____ m_____ C_____, w____ n_____

s_____, t___ b___ t_____ o_____

f_____ o_____ s_____, s____ t_____ w___ c_____ b___

m_____ r_____ w_____ G___t_____ C_____."

(2 C_____ 5:____ (NLT))

Day 5

Memorize Scripture. Using the first letter of each word in 2 Corinthians 5:21 (NLT) (*see* below), write out the verse from memory.

_____

_____

_____

_____

_____

"F G m C, w n s, t b t o f o s, s t w c b m r w G t C."

Chapter Notes. Pray and take time to reflect on God's faithfulness in making a way for us to have a relationship with Him. How has God been speaking to you this week? Take time to journal about what He has shown you.

_____

_____

_____

_____

_____

_____

_____

_____

WEEK 3

GROWING IN SPIRITUAL MATURITY

God loves you despite your flaws. And you can't do anything to make Him love you more or less. Yet, God loves you too much to leave you in the same condition in which you came to Him.

This week in chapter 3, we'll learn how God is faithful to change us into the image of Jesus. After you give your life to Him, God begins the work of purifying you. God uses the difficulties in your life—called trials in the Bible—to do that work.

Day 1

Pray and read chapter 3, pages 25 to 28 (stopping at the heading, *Revealing Trials*). Then answer the following questions based on what you've read.

1. Forgiveness of all sin is miraculous. Does that mean you have stopped sinning? _____

    Why not? _____

    _____

    _____

2. Is being tempted a sin? _____

    Read 1 Corinthians 10:13. What should you look for to overcome the temptation? _____

    _____

    _____

3. When you're in a relationship with God, you will begin to change. As you do, what do you begin to see more and less of in your life? _____

    _____

    _____

4. What does changing require from you? (Hint: *see* page 26, paragraph 2.) _____

    _____

    _____

    _____

5. How hard is it for you to let go of your dreams, goals, and desires to receive what God has planned for your life? _____

    _____

    _____

    _____

6. What does God use to grow us to spiritual maturity?

    _____

    _____

Memorize Scripture. Write out Jeremiah 18:4 (NKJV).

    _____

    _____

    _____

    _____

    _____

Day 2

Pray and read chapter 3, page 28 (starting at the **Revealing Trials** heading) to page 31 (stopping at the heading, **A Global Trial**). Then answer the following questions based on what you've read.

1. What is a "revealing trial"? _____

_____

_____

_____

_____

2. Has your faith been tested? _____

_____

How was it tested? _____

_____

_____

_____

_____

_____

_____

_____

What did the test reveal about your faith? _____

_____

_____

_____

_____

3. What is a "correcting trial"? _____

_____

_____

_____

_____

4. No one enjoys correction. But, according to Hebrews 12:11, what can be gained if a believer yields and receives God's correction? _____

_____

_____

5. What is a "perfecting trial"? _____

_____

_____

_____

_____

6. What can a believer expect from a perfecting trial?

_____

_____

_____

Memorize Scripture. Fill in the missing words to Jeremiah 18:4 (NKJV).

"And the _____ that _____ made of clay was _____ in the hand of the _____; so he made it again into _____ vessel, as it seemed _____ to the potter to make."

Day 3

Pray and read chapter 3, page 31 (starting at the heading, ***A Global Trial***) to page 38. Then answer the following questions based on what you've read.

1. What is a "global trial"? _____

_____

_____

_____

_____

2. What did God show you about yourself during the global trial? _____

_____

_____

_____

_____

_____

3. How did God use you to help others around you look to Him? _____

_____

_____

_____

_____

4. What does focusing on "what might have been" do? (Hint: *see* page 36.) _____

_____

5. List four things we can learn from going through trials.

_____

_____

_____

_____

Memorize Scripture. Fill in more missing words to Jeremiah 18:4 (NKJV).

"And the _____ that _____ made of _____ was _____ in the _____ of the _____; so he _____ it again into _____ _____, as it seemed _____ to the _____ to _____."

Day 4

Pray and answer the ***Going Deeper*** questions on pages 38 to 40.

Going Deeper 1. _____

_____

_____

_____

Going Deeper 2. _____

_____

_____

_____

_____

_____

Going Deeper 3. _____

_____

_____

_____

_____

_____

Going Deeper 4. _____

_____

_____

_____

_____

_____

_____

Memorize Scripture. Finish each word in this week's verse.

"A____ t____ v_____ t____ h__ m_____ o__

c_____ w___ m_____ i__ t____ h_____ o__

t___ p_____; s___ h__ m_____ i__ a_____

i_____ a_____ v_____, a___ i___ s_____

g_____ t__ t____ p_____ t__ m_____."

(J_____ 18:___ (NKJV))

Day 5

Memorize Scripture. Using the first letter of each word in Jeremiah 18:4 (NKJV) (*see* below), write out the verse from memory.

_____

_____

_____

_____

_____

_____

"A t v t h m o c w m i t h o t p; s h m i a i a v, a i s g t t p to m."

Chapter Notes. God can use trials to reveal to us what's in our hearts. What has God shown you about your heart as you've reflected this week on the trials you have gone through? Pray and take time to journal about the things God has revealed to you.

_____

_____

_____

_____

_____

_____

_____

_____

_____

_____

_____

_____

_____

_____

_____

_____

_____

_____

_____

_____

_____

_____

_____

_____

_____

_____

_____

_____

_____

_____

_____

_____

WEEK 4

THE GOOD SHEPHERD

Jesus is the good Shepherd. In chapter 4, we'll learn about God's faithfulness to provide for us, guide us, and protect us. As you read, think about the ways God has provided for, guided, and protected you.

Day 1

Pray and read chapter 4, pages 41 to 43. Then answer the following questions based on what you've read.

1. What animal are people compared to in different parts of the Bible? _____

   _____

2. List a sheep's vulnerabilities. _____

   _____

   _____

   _____

   _____

   _____

3. Whom do sheep need to survive? _____

   _____

   _____

   _____

   Why? _____

   _____

   _____

   _____

   _____

   _____

4. Without Jesus guiding you, you're left to your own devices. Which of the following examples can you relate to the most?

☐ Stubbornly follow the same paths even when it is harmful to me.

☐ Do things my friends do without first thinking about the consequences because I want to fit in and feel like I belong.

☐ Stray from doing what is right.

☐ Other: _____

5. As believers, what can we know as we follow the Good Shepherd? _____

_____

_____

_____

Memorize Scripture. Write out Ephesians 6:12 (NKJV).

_____

_____

_____

_____

_____

Day 2

Pray and read chapter 4, pages 44 to 48 (stopping at the *Guidance* heading). Then answer the following questions based on what you've read.

1. According to Philippians 4:19, what can you count on God to be faithful to provide for you? _____

    _____

    _____

2. Read Matthew 6:25. What does Jesus instruct you *not* to do when you have a need? _____

    _____

    In Matthew 6:33, what does Jesus instruct you to do instead? _____

    _____

    _____

3. How does Philippians 4:6-7 help you to practically apply Jesus' command to "seek first the Kingdom of God"? _____

    _____

    _____

4. What promise can you receive when you let go of worry and give God room to work in your life? _____

_____

_____

5. Do you have a "need" or a "want" that is causing you worry or that is making you anxious? Write it out here and pray to the One who can come through for you.

_____

_____

_____

_____

_____

_____

_____

Memorize Scripture. Fill in the missing words to Ephesians 6:12 (NKJV).

"For ____ do not wrestle against _____ and _____, but against principalities, against _____, against the rulers of the _____ of this age, against _____ hosts of wickedness in the _____ places."

Day 3

Pray and read chapter 4, page 48 (starting at the *Guidance* heading) to page 52 (stopping at the **Protection** heading). Then answer the following questions based on what you've read.

1. What has God given born-again believers to help guide us? _____

    _____

2. What are some of the truths and benefits we get from opening the Bible, God's Word? _____

    _____

    _____

    _____

    _____

    _____

3. What did you learn about the Holy Spirit's work in guiding us? _____

    _____

    _____

    _____

    _____

4. If God doesn't usually lead with signs and wonders, how does He reveal Himself to us according to 1 Kings 19:11-12? _____

_____

_____

Memorize Scripture Fill in more missing words to Ephesians 6:12 (NKJV).

"For ____ do not _____ against _____ and _____, but against _____, against _____, against the _____ of the _____ of this age, against _____ hosts of _____ in the _____ places."

Day 4

Pray and read chapter 4, page 52 (starting at the *Protection* heading) to page 58. Then answer the following questions based on what you've read.

1. As believers, from whom do we need protection?

_____

_____

2. According to John 10:10, what is Satan's mission that may cause you to fear? _____

_____

_____

_____

3. What two basic ways does fear manifest itself? _____

_____

_____

_____

4. Define the fear of the Lord. _____

_____

_____

_____

_____

_____

5. Define the fear of man or evil. _____

_____

_____

_____

_____

_____

6. What did Jesus do that defeated Satan and his demons and brought them under His subjection? _____

_____

_____

_____

_____

_____

Answer the *Going Deeper* questions on pages 58 to 61.

Going Deeper 1. _____

_____

_____

_____

_____

_____

Going Deeper 2. _____

_____

_____

_____

_____

Going Deeper 3. _____

_____

_____

_____

_____

_____

Going Deeper 4. _____

_____

_____

_____

_____

_____

Memorize Scripture. Finish each word in this week's verse.

"F____ w__ d__ n____ w_____ a_____
f_____ a____ b_____, b____ a_____
p_____, a_____ p_____, a_____
t____ r_____ o__ t____ d_____ o__ t____
a____, a_____ s_____ h____ o__ w_____
i__ t__ h_____ p_____." (E_____ 6:__
(NKJV))

Day 5

Memorize Scripture. Using the first letter of every word in the memory verse (*see* below), write out Ephesians 6:12 (NKJV) from memory.

_____

_____

_____

_____

_____

_____

"F w d n w a f a b, b a p, a p, a t r o t d o t a, a s h o w i t h p."

Chapter Notes. What has God revealed to you this week about His faithfulness in your life? Pray and take time to record what God has shown you.

_____

_____

_____

_____

_____

_____

_____

_____

WEEK 5

YIELDING TO THE GOOD SHEPHERD

When you learn about something God wants you to do, how quickly do you put it into practice? We can be stubborn and hold on to the things we want, refusing to let go. Or we can choose to open our hands so we can receive what God has for us.

By yielding your dreams, plans, and desires to your good Shepherd, Jesus, you'll be able to walk in the days He has made for you. As you read chapter 5 this week, ask God to show you the things in your life that He wants you to release to Him.

Day 1

Pray and read chapter 5, pages 63 to 64 (continuing through the end of the paragraph on page 65). Then answer the following questions based on what you've read.

1. Planning is wise, but what should your plans be subject to? _____

   Why? _____
   _____
   _____
   _____

2. In Psalm 37:4, what does it mean to "delight yourself in the Lord"? _____
   _____
   _____

   And, in that same verse, what does it mean that "He shall give you the desires of your heart"? _____
   _____
   _____
   _____
   _____

3. What desires has the Lord given you since surrendering your life to Him that you didn't have before? _____

_____

_____

_____

_____

_____

_____

4. According to Psalm 37:5, what command and promise come with committing your way to the Lord? _____

_____

_____

_____

_____

Memorize Scripture. Write out Proverbs 3:5-6 (NKJV).

_____

_____

_____

_____

_____

Day 2

Pray and read chapter 5, page 65 (starting at the first full paragraph) to page 67 (stopping at the end of the second full paragraph). Then answer the following questions based on what you've read.

1. Read Proverbs 3:5-6. What do those verses command you to do? _____

    _____

    _____

2. Rather than trying to figure out what God is going to do when He has not yet revealed something to you, how should you depend on Him? (Hint: *see* page 66.)

    _____

    _____

    _____

    _____

3. How can you make trusting God easier? _____

    _____

    _____

    _____

    _____

4. God's track record of faithfulness in our lives is 100%. Read 1 Thessalonians 5:23-24 in the New Living Translation. What does that verse reveal to you about God's character? _____

_____

_____

_____

_____

5. We're all inclined to live by leaning on our own understanding. Read Galatians 2:20. What perspective does that verse give you about your life as a Christian?

_____

_____

_____

_____

Memorize Scripture. Fill in the missing words in Proverbs 3:5-6 (NKJV).

"_____ in the _____ with all your _____, and lean not on your own _____; In all _____ ways acknowledge Him, and ____ shall _____ your _____."

Day 3

Pray and read chapter 5, page 67 (starting at the third full paragraph) to page 72. Then answer the following questions based on what you've read.

1. How do you respond when your plans don't work out?

    ☐ I stubbornly have a hard time letting go and continue trying to get my way.

    ☐ I seek the Lord for clarity and permission and wait for His leading.

    ☐ I accept the closed door, and I'm happily surprised when He works it out better than I expected.

2. What conclusion did the author come to when the fear of letting go overtook her? _____

    _____

    What are you afraid to let go of? _____

    _____

    _____

    _____

    _____

    _____

3. Read Psalm 32:8-10 in the New Living Translation. What does God promise to do for the godly? _____

_____

_____

_____

_____

_____

What are we not to act like? _____

_____

_____

Who is surrounded by unfailing love? _____

_____

_____

Memorize Scripture. Fill in more missing words to Proverbs 3:5-6 (NKJV).

"_____ in the _____ with _____ your _____,
and _____ not on _____ own _____;
In all _____ ways _____ Him, and _____
shall _____ your _____."

Day 4

Pray and answer the *Going Deeper* questions on pages 72 to 73.

Going Deeper 1. _____

_____

_____

_____

_____

_____

_____

Going Deeper 2. _____

_____

_____

_____

_____

_____

_____

_____

_____

_____

_____

Going Deeper 3. _____

_____

_____

_____

_____

_____

_____

_____

_____

_____

_____

_____

_____

Memorize Scripture. Finish each word in this week's verse.

"T_____ i__ t_____ L_____ w_____ a____ y_____

h_____; a____ l_____ n_____ o___ y_____ o_____

u_____; I___ a_____ y_____ w____

a_____ H_____, a____ H____ s_____ d_____

y_____ p_____." (P_____ 3:___-___ (NKJV))

Day 5

Memorize Scripture. Using the first letter of each word in the memory verse (*see* below), write out Proverbs 3:5-6 (NKJV) from memory.

_____

_____

_____

_____

_____

"T i t L w a y h, a l n o y o u; I a y w a H, a H s d y p."

Chapter Notes. Pray and take time to reflect on what God has shown you this week. Journal about what you learned about yourself.

_____

_____

_____

_____

_____

_____

_____

WEEK 6

DOING GOD'S WORK

God uses His people to reach other people. He could do His work on His own. God used a donkey to speak to Balaam (Numbers 22:28-30). And He spoke to Moses through a burning bush (Exodus 3:1-4).

God could do that all of the time. Yet, typically, God uses His people to reach others. Meditate on how God has worked in and through you to reach someone else as you read chapter 6 this week.

Day 1

Pray and read chapter 6, pages 75 to 81 (stopping at the *Power to Do God's Work* heading). Then answer the following questions based on what you've read.

1. What is needed to do God's work? _____

    _____

    _____

2. Simply put, what does it mean to abide in Jesus? _____

    _____

    _____

3. Think about where you are in your relationship with God today. Can people tell that you have been with Jesus by your lifestyle? _____

    How? _____

    _____

    _____

    _____

    _____

    _____

4. Take a few moments to reflect on what your "heart motivation" has been lately. Is it drawing you closer to Jesus or further away from Him? _____

_____

_____

_____

_____

_____

_____

5. What does it mean "to be present with Jesus"? _____

_____

_____

_____

_____

_____

6. What does God promise to do when you draw near to Him? _____

_____

_____

_____

Memorize Scripture. Write out Psalm 16:8 (NKJV).

_____

_____

_____

_____

_____

Day 2

Pray and read chapter 6, page 81 (starting at the *Power to Do God's Work* heading) to page 84 (stopping at the *God Prepares You* heading). Then answer the following questions based on what you've read.

1. Part of abiding in Jesus is to be a doer of His word. How do we do that as believers? _____

_____

_____

_____

2. Have you experienced the empowering work of the Spirit in your life? _____

How? _____

_____

_____

_____

_____

3. Where does part of that power come from? _____

_____

_____

_____

_____

_____

4. When doing God's work, what should you remember not to do? (Hint: *see* page 82.) _____

_____

_____

5. If God prepares the way, how should you respond when God tells you to do something? (Hint: *see* page 83.) _____

_____

_____

Memorize Scripture. Fill in the missing words in Psalm 16:8 (NKJV).

"I have _____ the Lord _____ before me;

_____ He is at my _____ hand I shall

_____ be moved."

Day 3

Pray and read chapter 6, page 84 (starting at the ***God Prepares You*** heading) to page 92. Then answer the following questions based on what you've read.

1. How does God equip us to do His work? _____

    _____

2. Do you know what your primary spiritual gift is? _____

    What is your spiritual gift and how are you exercising it in the body of Christ? _____

    _____

    _____

    _____

    _____

3. A servant must be faithful. Give examples of how you have invested God's resources, your talents, for His glory. _____

_____

_____

_____

_____

_____

_____

_____

_____

_____

4. Take time to examine yourself. How do you typically respond when the Lord prompts you to do something?

☐ With fear and anxiousness, eventually talking myself out of obedience.

☐ With many questions and seeking confirmation before moving forward.

☐ With faith and trust that God will tell me what to do along the way.

Memorize Scripture. Fill in more missing words in Psalm 16:8 (NKJV).

"___ have _____ the _____ _____ before ____;
_____ _____ is at _____ _____ hand
I shall _____ be _____."

Day 4

Pray and answer the ***Going Deeper*** questions on pages 92 to 93.

Going Deeper 1. _____

_____

_____

_____

_____

_____

_____

_____

_____

_____

_____

_____

y..Chapter 6

Going Deeper 2. _____

_____

_____

_____

_____

_____

_____

Going Deeper 3. _____

_____

_____

_____

_____

_____

Memorize Scripture. Finish each word in this week's verse.

"I h_____ s____ t____ L_____ a_____ b_____

m___; B_____ H___ i____ a___ m___ r_____

h____ I s_____ n____ b__ m_____." (P_____

16:___ (NKJV))

67

Day 5

Memorize Scripture. Using the first letter of every word in Psalm 16:8 (NKJV) (*see* below), write out the verse from memory.

_____

_____

_____

_____

_____

"I h s t L a b m; B H i a m r h I s n b m."

Chapter Notes. How has God been speaking to you this week as you've learned about His faithfulness in helping you to do His work? Pray and journal about what you have learned and how it has impacted you.

_____

_____

_____

_____

_____

_____

WEEK 7

WALKING BY FAITH WITH GOD

You have a choice. You can walk by faith. Or you can walk by sight.

Walking by sight can result in a roller coaster of emotions. If something good happens in your life, you feel happy. But if things aren't going so well, you get depressed.

In contrast, walking by faith is a process of trusting God regardless of life's circumstances. It's knowing that God is in control of everything in your life and believing that He will do whatever is best for you.

Meditate on God's trustworthiness as you read chapter 7 this week.

Day 1

Pray and read chapter 7, pages 95 to 101 (stopping at the *You Are a New Creation in Christ* heading). Then answer the following questions based on what you've read.

1. As Christians, how are we to walk? _____

_____

Why? _____

_____

_____

_____

_____

2. Who can we rely on in every circumstance? _____

_____

Why? _____

_____

_____

_____

_____

3. What does "walking by faith" mean? _____

_____

_____

_____

_____

_____

4. The people listed in Hebrews 11 were what kind of people? _____

_____

_____

5. What helps us to walk by faith and not by what we see?

_____

_____

_____

6. What does the word "dayenu" mean? _____

_____

_____

_____

_____

_____

What promise of God can you add to dayenu? _____

_____

_____

_____

_____

_____

_____

Memorize Scripture. Write out Hebrews 11:6 (NKJV).

_____

_____

_____

_____

_____

Day 2

Pray and read chapter 7, page 101 (starting at the *You Are a New Creation in Christ* heading) to page 103 (stopping at the *God is Working All Things Together for Good* heading). Then answer the following questions based on what you've read.

1. As a new creation in Christ, list the noticeable changes that have taken place in your life.

Old Life Attitudes/Practices	New Life Attitudes/Practices
Lied to get out of trouble	Tell the truth to honor God
_____	_____
_____	_____
_____	_____
_____	_____
_____	_____
_____	_____
_____	_____
_____	_____

2. How does knowing that God has wash**ed** you, sanctifi**ed** you, and justifi**ed** you encourage you to endure and persevere through the process of living as a new creation? _____

_____

_____

_____

_____

_____

_____

_____

_____

3. What promise can we count on by faith even when we don't "feel" God's presence? _____

_____

_____

Memorize Scripture. Fill in the missing words in Hebrews 11:6 (NKJV).

"But without faith it is _____ to please _____, for he who _____ to God must _____ that He is, and that He is a _____ of those who _____ seek Him."

Day 3

Pray and read chapter 7, page 103 (starting at the *God is Working All Things Together for Good* heading) to page 107. Then answer the following questions based on what you've read.

1. What does it mean that God works "all" things together for good? _____

_____

_____

What does it *not* mean? _____

_____

_____

_____

_____

2. When, by faith, we count on God's promise to work all things together for good, what can we prevent from happening to us? _____

_____

_____

_____

_____

3. How does the promise that Jesus is preparing a place for you help you to prepare to be with Him? _____

_____

_____

_____

_____

_____

_____

_____

4. What does having eternal life consist of? (Hint: *see* page 107.) _____

   _____

   _____

   _____

5. According to Revelation 21:4, what will not be part of eternal life that we experience now in this life? _____

   _____

   _____

   _____

   _____

   _____

Memorize Scripture. Fill in more missing words in Hebrews 11:6 (NKJV).

"But _____ faith it is _____ to please _____, for he who _____ to _____ must _____ that He ____, and that He is a _____ of those who _____ _____ Him."

Day 4

Pray and answer the *Going Deeper* questions on pages 108 to 109. Then read the *Afterword* on pages 111 to 113.

Going Deeper 1. _____

_____

_____

_____

_____

_____

_____

_____

Going Deeper 2. _____

_____

_____

_____

_____

_____

_____

_____

Going Deeper 3. _____

_____
_____
_____
_____
_____
_____
_____
_____
_____
_____
_____

Memorize Scripture. Finish each word in this week's verse.

"B___ w_____ f_____ i___ i___ i_____
t____ p_____ H_____, f____ h___ w_____ c_____
t____ G____ m_____ b_____ t_____ H___ i____,
a____ t_____ H___ i___ a r_____ o__ t_____
w___ d_____ s_____ H_____."(H_____
11:___ (NKJV))

Day 5

Memorize Scripture. Using the first letter of each word in Hebrews 11:6 (NKJV) (*see* below), write out the verse from memory.

_____

_____

_____

_____

_____

_____

"B w f i i i t p H, f h w c t G m b t H i, a t H i a r o t w d s H."

Chapter Notes. Pray and take time to meditate on God's promises that you learned about this week. Journal about what God has impressed upon your heart in knowing that He will be faithful to fulfill them.

_____

_____

_____

_____

_____

_____

_____

STREAMING VIDEO ACCESS

The book and study guide may also be used along with seven video teachings that you can access for free. If you plan to use the video teachings, the study works best when the participants read the chapter and complete the study guide in the week before the video teaching is shown.

Then, as a group, the following format is encouraged:

- Welcome prayer.

- Worship.

- Video teaching.

- Small group prayer: break out into groups of three to four people and pray for ten minutes about prayer points focused on the week's material.

- Study group time: break out into groups of ten or fewer people. The smaller groups will give all of the participants an opportunity to share and help encourage a good discussion. Remember to start your group time with prayer to invite God into your discussion time.

You can access the video teachings by going to WalkByFaithWithGod.com/ebenezer-stones-teaching-videos or by using the QR code:

Ebenezer Stones
Streaming Teaching Videos